FISCHER

TORTURED IN THE PASADENA JAILHOUSE

(featuring THE MORALS OF CHESS by Benjamin Franklin)

FEATURING *THE MORALS OF CHESS*
BY BENJAMIN FRANKLIN

F
I
S
C
H
E
R

TORTURED IN THE PASADENA JAILHOUSE

J. M. ROCK

For the raw-boned individual,
the one who thinks for himself, who lives deliberately and
makes his moves with a certain readiness to defend them.

*The greatest threat to liberty is the aspiration
to define its terms.*

It is up to you to keep them in its favor.

Ad libertas,

CONTENTS

ABOUT THE AUTHOR

Born just north of Detroit, Michigan, Jonathan Michael Rock is an author, economist, historian and philosopher dedicated to the cause of liberty. As the founder and author of Paradocracy.com, Mr. Rock draws on his extensive research and his personal experience in fields both public and private, ranging from the armed forces, subsidized housing, real estate, and social work to financial services, business intelligence, and the mortgage industry.

Apart from his career, his endless research and the hundreds of articles he has written, Mr. Rock is an avid adventurer, traveler, musician, athlete, mountaineer, Civil War reenactor, chess enthusiast, and collector of historical artifacts and Americana. Proud of his American heritage and way of life, he spends his time with his family on his ranch in the shadows of the Sierra Nevada, usually donning a Stetson. In all of his writings, his objectives are clear: to advance the cause of liberty, to resist the tides of tyranny, to discover and deliver the truth, and, above all, to leave his heirs and posterity better prepared to defend and exercise their inalienable rights.

Mr. Rock published his treatise *Death by Socialism* in 2024.

INTRODUCTION

BY J. M. ROCK

The name Bobby Fischer reigns supreme in the world of chess, yet there was a time when it hogged headlines, when it struck fear into the eyes of the competition, when it was on the lips of folks all across the globe. More than the face of the centuries-old game, there was a time when Bobby Fischer was synonymous with the cause and the spirit of America, that his moves on the chessboard sought more than checkmate but to pit the strength of "raw-boned American individualism" against "the Soviet megalithic system" which had come to dominate the game of chess as it had done also at the time within the realm of Cold War politics. Fischer's triumph over the Soviet Union's Boris Spassky in the 1972 World Chess Championship would ultimately be celebrated as a symbolic and diplomatic victory for the United States, but, as time would tell, it would not mean the American dream for the man himself.

The name Bobby Fischer is synonymous with chess and genius, yet for those who have ever cared to know the man, the intellect and the personality, his name is one of great mystery and legend. Fischer was a larger-than-life figure whose life story proves the point: whether it be his controversial opinions on matters of politics, his traumatic experiences at the Pasadena Jailhouse, or his life of exile in Iceland, throughout his life Fischer remained true to himself and his convictions regardless of the threats or the consequences. He remained Bobby Fischer until the very hour of his death in Reykjavík, Iceland, on January 17, 2008, when he perished at the age of sixty-four, his age equalling the number of squares on a chessboard.

This book, *Fischer: Tortured in the Pasadena Jailhouse*, reproduces the original text written by Fischer in June of 1981 (and later self-published in 1982), documenting the "incredible and absolutely true events" of his arrest and torture in Pasadena, California, between May 26 and May 28 of 1981. The text offers a glimpse not only into the aguish of a brilliant man, not only into the harrowing circumstances which beset one of the greatest thinkers of his time; it is written testament to the long history of abuse suffered at the hands of unchecked and arrogant authority, the plight of a thinking man in a 'civilized' society — the kind of 'civilized' society distinguished for its thoughtless obedience and its expectation of conformity.

Fischer's text is followed by Benjamin Franklin's *The Morals of Chess* as a means to capturing the characteristics of the player who masters the game of chess, who appreciates the special qualities of a game emulating the aspects of life itself. Fischer's text is preceded by the writings of J. M. Rock, the author of *Death by Socialism*, as a means to priming the reader to receive Fischer's message in its proper context, and to relate his experiences and the themes of his writing to more recent and relatable events, and thus to enable the reader to truly appreciate the implications of such a society tolerant of abuse.

It is in this way that *Fischer: Tortured in the Pasadena Jailhouse* serves not only as a time capsule but as a palpable reminder of the classic clash between man and machine, the latter in this case being the machinery of the state which claims to be the master of all men.

Ultimately, this story represents the thinking man's plight against the conventions, his yearning to be valued and respected where he already knows he will never be truly understood, where all too often any public appreciation of events tends to favor the forces against him, the forces against critical and independent thought, and ultimately the forces against truth: forces taking the form of government, the establishment, the (new or existing) status quo; the problem with the human condition being such that, in one's desire to understand (or in his attempt to curb his outrage, to relieve himself of any moral obligation to his fellow man, and to justify his continued complacency about his situation), the bystander inherently finds himself seeking a justification even for the unjustifiable, the absolutely "incredible" and unspeakable kinds of injustices which are beyond basic understanding or simply too disturbing for the sensitive stomachs of people with little tolerance for unsettling facts.

It is due to these facts of life that genius tends toward a state of utter desperation, loneliness, few allies yet various opponents, and perhaps why the likes of Bobby Fischer possess such extremes of *foresight, circumspection, caution,* and *perseverance,* and why, as Benjamin Franklin so eloquently put it in *The Morals of Chess,* the game itself "is not merely an idle amusement" but "the image of human life… and war"; the latter often being a war between men actively ridding their minds of contradictions and others who make a living from defending theirs.

FOREWORD

BY J. M. ROCK

W hen a people have succumbed to tyranny, the punishment doled out assumes a certain quality, a kind of official capacity, business as usual.

Not only do the 'officials' come to view their egos as one of their leading qualifications, one of the basic job requirements, they come to view their hostility as one of the *primary* requirements, one of the most reliable tools on their belts, their preferred tool for any task. Indeed, that general hostility, the heavy hand of government, has become part of the very archetype of the 'professional law enforcement officer', business as usual for that institution maintaining a monopoly over the initiation of force and coercion; that institution specializing in torment, torture, intimidation and trauma, often to the point of permanent bodily damage and occasionally to the point of death, all in pursuit of social paralysis (or assuring the public's obedience) in the name of 'official business'.

Indeed, the 'officials' and the 'enforcers' come to view their hostility, disrespect and their generally unpleasant, dismissive and insulting demeanors as entitlements, perks of the job and proof of authority, badges of courage and benefits of the offices they hold: the kinds of insulting attitudes forming part of the culture, being accepted as fair treatment for those questioned, detained, or apprehended, and the kinds of offices regarded internally as superior to those assumed by mere 'civilians' who, in the view of the bureaucracy, are best assumed inferior in intellect, lousy at life, and guilty until proven innocent; 'civilians' who are apparently entitled to nothing near the sort of respect or dutiful reverence they are expected at all times to extend eagerly to their masters; 'civilians' who are considered 'disorderly' or 'interfering' or 'resisting' or 'mentally ill' — or, another favorite, 'nutty Constitutionalists' — for articulating their disapproval or for daring to defend their rights; 'civilians' who are often at the receiving end of threats and hostility (and even fabricated charges) for their refusal or even their mere reluctance to submit, obey, or grovel to the satisfaction of the 'officer', the 'enforcer' carrying a badge, a loaded gun, and a loaded ego, prepared to use all three to have his way; 'civilians' who are, apparently, constantly getting in the way and never paying enough in the way of taxes for the privilege of occupying so much space, enjoying the benefits of so much 'progress', and being the loyal subjects of such 'civilized' society, whose enforcers of 'civility' enjoy both the unique privilege of conducting their own 'internal investigations' and the protection of 'qualified immunity' (and paid leave) wherever the bureaucracy is even prepared to admit the possibility of a mistake. What's more, where fellow members of that bureaucracy are to witness any 'mistake' or transgression, whether in the form of violated procedure or in the form of ill-treatment, members are behooved by peer pressure (or by the threat of losing their jobs) to ignore it or to turn and walk away if not actively supporting the enforcers. What a twisted idea of 'civility' we have.

Facing little resistance and rarely a penalty for any 'mistakes' made in the course of their 'duties', the members of the bureaucracy come to view the hostility toward, and manhandling of, the public as part of their day-to-day; and the people are expected to accept these as part of theirs, too, only on the receiving end, should they be suspected of causing any 'disturbance', 'discomfort', or 'interference' (or generally any inconvenience to the establishment), regardless of whether any citizen is within his rights. Meanwhile, the people themselves come to fear being trampled by this massive bureaucracy of bullies, the weight of which stands to crush more than the man himself, but his very soul.

Indeed, the weight of big government ultimately becomes so unbearable that even the most battle-hardened warriors come to fear it over death itself. As Pvt. David Kenyon Webster described his time in the U. S. Army during World War II, they are "more afraid of defying the authority of an officer, backed up by the whole Army and a court-martial composed of officers like him, than we are of death by shell fire." He continued: "Discipline is fear, not leadership, and we are afraid — not of [the officer] but of the irresistible force that he represents. Afraid for our lives, we are more afraid of the system that holds us in thrall, and so we lie here and wait to be killed, because an officer tells us to lie here." This is the state of the soldier "in thrall" as it is the state of things under the weight of any massive bureaucracy or tyranny of any kind.

Always waiting for the next shoe to drop, man and woman alike come to anticipate the punches before they're even delivered, taking solace in being spared and even scoffing at those who cause any disruption: those who don't anticipate the abuse or who dare to dodge the punches or even strike back. Likewise, the people do whatever they can to avoid persecution and the hefty costs (fines, legal fees, jail time, court appearances, humiliation) of defending themselves — from the kinds of bullies indifferent to the public, accustomed to toying with the people's rights, feeding their own massive but fragile egos, or simply 'doing their jobs', making sure to protect their incomes and benefits, to prioritize (at virtually all costs) their safety, their job security and the handsome pensions promised at the end of their careers (granted only if they continue to play along and do as they're told).

Persecuting at their will and selectively at their own discretion, the members of the bureaucracy are restrained in their political activities in name only. Although ostensibly forbidden by federal edict (under the Hatch Act), federal agents and bureaucrats all over actively advance their own political causes, or the prevailing causes of the establishment, by determining what actually qualifies as 'political' and what constitutes 'official business', what is 'progressive' and what is 'politically-correct', what is 'insensitive' and 'inappropriate', and ultimately which 'laws' they enforce, which 'crimes' they prosecute, and which ones they either don't know or let slide. In other words, they pursue their political causes all the same by deciding how and whom to persecute; what 'crimes' are worth prosecuting and which 'criminals' are worth charging; what constitutes extenuating (or aggravating) circumstances and what doesn't; which activities are worth tolerating and which are decidedly unfit for 'civilized' society; or, on the whole, which policies and which practices serve the interests of the establishment and which ones threaten to undermine or disturb it.

In the course of this despotism wrapping its tentacles ever tighter around the public, the people come to pay for their further humiliation and subjugation, the militarization and empowerment of these forces against them.

Likewise, the people come to expect ever greater force and coercion from the enforcers: mistreatment, threats, hostility, heavy-handedness and even outright torture from the bullies who are 'just doing their jobs' and consistently underestimating the threats they pose to the country (or the community) they claim to serve; the country they claim to be so patriotic about (without having any substantial knowledge of its history, its traditions, or its constitution). Of course, this is a twisted (and hollow) form of 'patriotism' in service to government, in service to the state, the usurpers, not the kind of patriotism of the American tradition which serves the interests and liberties of the people.

This is, perhaps, the only manner in which the bullies are consistent: seldom ever consistent in matters of logic, ethics, or morality — these types of 'consistency' being feasible only outside of the master-slave relationship — they are nearly always prepared to justify suspending the rights of man, doing so callously without any regard for the constitution they swear to uphold, without any regard for the preciousness of the particular article of freedom upon which they so casually tread in the course of their regular 'duties'. Likewise, the people succumbing to this tyranny come to regard their liberties in the same way, not as rights inherited from their Creator but privileges afforded them (often arbitrarily) by the grace and mercy of any given member of the state; members often operating from their own kinds of god complex, or an inferiority complex met with the means to seek retribution and take out their own personal frustrations on the people whom they envy or regard with disdain (or whom they otherwise bless with their indifference).

Even in the face of the absurd, the humiliating, and the most abject of inhumanities, witnesses and victims alike are hardly fazed by the force, the violence and the arrogance of 'public servants' in their dealings with the public, especially among those enforcers who present themselves more like soldiers chomping at the bit in front of their number-one enemy, the people (and their rights); people whom the enforcers would much rather see just hurry up and die; people who even come to wish this upon themselves after such ill-treatment, who come to expect pain and discomfort from the bureaucracy, who expect agony for any individual among them having the misfortune of encountering any enforcer in the course of his regular 'duties' or his ongoing 'investigation'. Indeed, the people even extend their gratitude where they are spared, and the bullies — who expect desperate pleas from the people, the benefactors responsible for their salaries (apparently for the privilege of licking boots and taking punishment) — even take some measure of pride when they manage to squeeze that gratitude out of their 'suspects'; every citizen, every benefactor having the privilege of being assumed a 'suspect' until cleared of wrongdoing.

A people succumbing to tyranny will be terrorized by even the very possibility of offending the bureaucracy, so much so that even a mere letter in the mail, bearing some official letterhead, is enough to send the citizen into a full-blown panic attack, to convince the citizen that he is a criminal or that he threatens to become one should he fail to do his duty and pay his respects to the state. The citizen will beg and plead for mercy, apologizing to the bullies for his mere existence, his daring to even consider the possibility of freedom, his daring to fancy himself worthy of such a prize as free will, human rights, and personal discretion, his daring to call himself an American endowed with these qualities, his daring to exercise and affirm his inalienable rights or to merely consider himself innocent until proven guilty. Under such tyranny, it is at his own risk that any citizen considers himself anything other than a criminal, a blight upon humanity, a corrupting and contaminating force requiring corrections and remediation.

As far as the bullies in the bureaucracy see it, the people are free from torture only through its grace and mercy; the people being accountable to its every whim, weakened and emasculated to the point of complete and unquestioning (and even proud) obedience, even to the point of condemning peers who present legitimate grievances or disputes, with the people generally doing their best to avoid being railroaded and crushed by the weight of a thoughtless and heartless bureaucracy. Of course, in the view of those within the bureaucracy (and those con-doning it), this isn't 'torture' at all, just business as usual. It is a sick and twisted state, indeed, wherever the people, any society, has succumbed to this disease, wherever this plague is said to be the mark of 'civilized' society, wherever the contagion is presented as the cure, and wherever the individual is considered 'crazy' or 'insane' or 'mentally-ill' or 'dangerous to society' for challenging any of this or merely pointing any of it out.

ONE OF EVERY THREE AMERICAN ADULTS IS A CRIMINAL

BY J. M. ROCK

In 2014, *The Wall Street Journal* reported on the growing epidemic of criminal records among Americans; this preceding the sudden outbreak of violence and widespread looting amid the riots, misguided protests, shoplifting sprees and crimes of opportunity following the 2020 death of George Floyd while under arrest in Minneapolis, Minnesota; this preceding the extremes of *sanctuary cities*, politically-motivated race riots and looting, lax attitudes toward *real* crime, the growing indifference toward the most basic of standards for ethics, morality, community, and decency, the kinds of degeneracy (or calculated subversion) specifically brought about or tolerated by the government agencies themselves which are charged with serving the public, or which assert that case, but which so regularly fail in their stated duties, albeit often by design.

Consider the State of California, which, as of 2014, classifies theft of items worth $950 or less as a *misdemeanor*, with many prosecutors across the state refusing, in such cases, to prosecute and many police departments refusing to book these criminals or even make arrests; and where they *do* make arrests, they often release the criminals down the street or elsewhere in the city. In the wake of the horrific 2025 Palisades Fire, consider the crimes committed by the 'homeless population', a group consisting primarily of psychopaths, sociopaths, junkies, and addicts who've burned more than proverbial bridges with the people in their lives, the landlords who've housed them, and the employers who've hired them. According to the *Los Angeles Times* in an article regarding the first quarter of 2021, "[Homelessness-related fires made] up fifty-four percent of all fires the department responded to"; that figure leaps to eighty percent when considering downtown Los Angeles for the whole of 2021.

And so it's statistically likely and widely speculated that the flames sweeping through Southern California at the time of this writing were started by that same population: a 'homeless' or 'unhoused' population not only condemning themselves to their stations in life but incentivized and subsidized (through food stamps, Social Security payments, and housing allowances) and even supplied with drugs by, you guessed it, the government. Even when a blowtorch-wielding vagrant (and illegal immigrant) was spotted by half a dozen witnesses and detained by private citizens when attempting to set fire to old Christmas trees during the most destructive fire in Los Angeles history, police brought the suspect down to the station then only a few hours later released him back onto the streets. 'Officials' said that there was no *probable cause* to charge him with arson, despite the half a dozen witnesses who saw him setting things on fire and the guy having a blowtorch on him when they arrested him. According to the bureaucrats in Los Angeles, apparently, that's just not *probable cause*.

However, much lesser 'offenses' are often met with far harsher penalties with far less evidence, even no evidence at all; and, of course, where the most criminal of negligence takes places, among powerful political actors, there are seldom ever any consequences as a result. With this level of political incompetence, let alone the mismanagement of California's fire-prone forests, the mismanagement of public utilities and infrastructure, the mismanagement of water resources and reservoirs which would have otherwise been available for fighting the fires, it is not at all surprising that many attribute this catastrophe to negligence within government, to a government with its priorities out of whack, even to sinister motives within an establishment of political actors paying no personal price for the disasters but standing to benefit in the way of clearing the land to serve its future plans.

Again, it has to make you wonder just how much of this is by design, in service to the obvious or still other agendas yet to be known — a design enabling police officers to tread where they are unwelcome, condemning them to fail in the duties they are actually expected to perform, and yet, as if by some miracle, getting the public to cede progressively more power so they can finally get around to doing what they were supposed to be doing all along, or so they promise. Put slightly differently, it is in this way that the state manages to do that which it is not authorized to do, that it manages to not do that which it is supposed to be doing, and yet that it still manages to convince the public that the police need additional resources and authority to do more. This kind of insanity is enough to make your head spin, enough to make you wonder who the real criminals are in this case.

Returning to the aforementioned article, in 2014 *The Wall Street Journal* reported that nearly one out of every three American adults has a criminal record, roughly equaling the number of Americans who have a college degree; a statistic corroborated in 2014, and still supported in 2025, by the Federal Bureau of Investigation (FBI), whose records show more than seventy million individuals on file within the organization's master criminal database.

One can't help but wonder: Is this an indication of a society which has simply become more innately predisposed to violence and criminal activity over the long run, or is it also (or even more so) the symptom of a society in decay and under the influence, literally as much as figuratively?

Consider the restrictions imposed by ever more red tape, the kinds thwarting enterprise, independence, and human ambition; the kinds of "red tape and paperwork and requirements of the ICC, the PSC, the OCC, the ACC, FICA, IRS and so forth," as described by Frank Campbell of the old Campbell 66 Express (of Route 66), which ultimately put an end to his decades-old freight-hauling business in 1986, after, as Campbell put it, "It got so a truck couldn't move until the weight of the paperwork equalled the weight of the load."

Consider the society oppressed by irresponsible economic policies, attitudes encouraging isolation and anxiety, helplessness and subordination; attitudes discouraging or prohibiting the kinds of relationships, initiative and investments, both tangible and intangible, that make for and sustain fruitful and fulfilling living.

Consider the systemic disadvantages suffered in the name of political expedience, 'political correctness' or 'the common good'; disadvantages which fuel dissatisfaction and resentment, real or perceived 'injustices', 'inequities' and 'inequalities' driving peaceful or not-so-peaceful protests, and consider the public 'education' systems failing students in their curricula and promoting disruptive narratives specifically enabling those of the perceived variety, those suggesting that the fates of the students are predetermined by such factors beyond their control.

Consider the types of incentives upon a people in such a society where making an unintelligible political fuss becomes a way of life and a kind of career, a way to seek fame, fortune, or 'entitlements'; each a type of grift exploiting the weaknesses and sensibilities of the public. Consider the society overburdened by onerous and cumbersome laws, ordinances, and regulations, the society in decline due to moral hazard, untenable debt and unfunded liabilities, the destructive incentives of the burgeoning welfare state (and such an aggravating state strictly incompatible with a state of liberty).

Consider the related rise in single-parent households, the rise of "free-love" doctrines in defiance of "Family," as Henry Ford is known to have put it, "… the old-fashioned loyalty of one man and one woman to each other and their children — [this being] the basis not only of society, but of all personal character and progress."

The statistical implications for those raised without one of the two parents, especially those lacking fathers, are devastating, even forgetting the gross effects of other youths raised essentially without parents but through

daycare centers and public schools so that parents can par-
take in that society governed progressively by money matters, the unfulfilling kind of 'getting' instead of 'making',
not only for objects and status desired but for the sake of
those parents keeping their homes and their peace of mind
as they avoid penalty or jail time for failing to meet their
liabilities to the state. Consider the attitudes of parents on
matters of child abuse and spanking, the 'social' attitudes
which condone these cruelties, the types of abuses priming
children to tolerate the abuses of 'authorities' ruling over
them; priming children to view themselves as the subjects
within a continued master-slave relationship, with those
children themselves eventually becoming the parents who
continue that sorry tradition; a 'tradition' priming children to view the state as some paternal figure and enabling
women to view it as a substitute for husbands, who, in a
twist of irony, constitute the larger share of the tax base.

Consider the results of these, not limited to gang
activity, violent behavior, low income, professional and
academic underperformance, financial and functional
illiteracy, mental illness, drug dependency and abuse
(and consequent 'homelessness'); and consider the effects
of these on behavior and relationships, and the political
consequences in the form of voting patterns among these
demographics (including the single parents themselves):
those voting patterns in support of state-sponsored (and

authoritarian) 'solutions' to problems they don't understand, problems exacerbated or even created by the institutions in which they (knowingly or otherwise) place
their faith and which they empower to make things much
worse, ironically through the enforcement mechanism
of the very police officers whom they slander, resent and
mistrust for (many or mostly) incoherent reasons, officers
who, as shown, are certainly worthy of sharp scrutiny and
(in many cases) even contempt.

Consider the disdain for human initiative and industry, whether it be out of spite and jealousy, a desperate
desire to make an intellectual or moral case for their indo-
lence, or 'justified' by doctrine and dogma masquerading
as 'science'; the kind of 'science' wielded to 'justify' scold-
ing their opponents whom they regard as lowly bumpkins
unqualified to speak on such serious matters. That is, of
course, when they themselves (the ones casting disdain)
lack any specific qualifications or articulable evidence (that
they understand) to support their claims.

Consider the growing disregard for the sanctity of
human life, especially that disregard for the lives of the
unborn (not unrelated to feminist, Leftist politics).
Consider the desensitization of the population to violence,
criminal activity, even war, torture and murder, an outcome not without some influence by media and propa-
ganda, the influence of a society both out of touch with

the physical world and ever more disconnected from the realities of such extremes as combat and genuine suffering. Consider the establishment condemning initiative, championing victimhood, politicizing matters of probity and property, confounding simple facts and principles of personal responsibility, and condoning large-scale theft and violence (in the present and in futurity) as a means to 'social justice', 'economic reform', 'equality', or 'reparations'.

In a country whose growing numbers depend upon government (i.e. taxpayers and foreign creditors) for their salaries, subsidies, and *entitlements*, the relationship between man and state has essentially been compromised, with hardly a man ready or willing to challenge the hand which ostensibly feeds him, which thereby so charitably permits his survival, which establishment has managed to permit him to keep whatever he possesses in the way of property or peace of mind. This is indeed the means by which a cruel relationship between abuser and dependent is facilitated, encouraged and maintained; the abuse defending the system which promises the plenty, with the promises, being popular enough and politically unimpeachable, in turn appearing to justify the abuse.

It is through this circular phenomenon, this wretched system which mechanically dehumanizes and distances the people from their governments and each other, that the people's acquiescence is virtually guaranteed, and ultimately it is in this way, among others, that the people are quite literally *bought and paid for* in their submission to the state, in their tolerance for being treated as criminals, and in their political assault upon the rights and property of their fellow man. For this reason alone, ignoring the fear, ignorance, indifference and avarice of an increasingly-un-principled society of incompetents and malcontents, many are apparently more than willing to surrender progressively more of their freedom, or that which remains of it, for the promise of free stuff; a certain culture within (and a growing segment of) society strictly incompatible with a state of liberty and, put differently, other cultures within that society that place a value on honor and integrity, character and respect, morals and ethics, initiative and personal responsibility, pride and patriotism; this known incompatibility perhaps forming one basis for the political initiatives promoting open borders specifically and multiculturalism more generally, thereby forming the basis for further *enforcement* and *regulation* where the people had previously preserved their civility through the congenial character of their communities. Of course, this also manages to pit the people against each other, to enable the establishment to divide and conquer (physically as well as intellectually); and, especially where it maintains the illusion of a democratic system, this manages to convince the people that the excessive powers of the state are not to be challenged but rather embraced; that these oppressive forces can even benefit their cause. Indeed, if only they can bolster their ranks and rally enough support at the ballot box, they can use the force of the establishment to pummel their enemies into submission; of course, this kind of abuse through government seldom being ruled 'criminal' and scarcely ever being called to account for the crimes committed.

In any event, the thirty-three percent (or so) of Americans who are classified as 'criminals' are 'criminals' in a country not lacking the initiative to bequeath this distinction upon ever more of its citizens. Indeed, members of the state are constantly concocting new schemes and initiatives: in fact, the page count of the Code of Federal Regulations (CFR) alone has increased from 71,224 to over 200,000 during the fifty years between 1975 and 2025. Along with the perverse and pervasive proliferation of laws across the United States, their enforcement has become progressively more aggressive and egregious; that is, of course, wherever and on whichever occasions officers elect to enforce them. Meanwhile, the incidence of police brutality, along with the subversion of Constitutional rights which comes with it, has become more obvious and abhorrent, more frequent and flagrant, more brazen and daring. What's more, as previously explained, this threat to the Constitutional (and inherent) rights of Americans is becoming ever more serious over time.

Many activists, journalists, social media pages, and online publications, such as those found through *The Free Thought Project*, populate the web virtually every day with accounts of government misconduct. Other websites, such as Reason.com, regularly document these violent incidents. As we have observed in such cases as the 1992 siege on the Weaver family home in Ruby Ridge, Idaho, the 1993 siege on the Branch Davidians in Waco, Texas, and the 2016 killing of Tony Timpa, the police state has laid siege upon the people systematically and often indifferently, without much in the way of second thoughts.

In the case of Tony Timpa, he was an unarmed man who called 9-1-1 for assistance during a mental break-down, informing the dispatcher that he had schizophrenia and depression but had not taken his prescription medication. To repeat, it was he who had called 9-1-1 for assistance yet was instead issued a death sentence in effect, that taking the form of homicide from "the stress of being restrained" by police officers in Dallas, Texas; that occurring after Timpa (who had already been restrained by a security officer by the time police had arrived on scene) had lost consciousness, after repeatedly crying out, "You're gonna kill me!", and after the police on scene restrained Timpa, holding him prone on grass for nearly fourteen minutes with his legs zip-tied and one officer pressing his knee into Timpa's back.

Readers may also consider such events as those from 2014 in Ferguson, Missouri, where we witnessed the power of a heavily-militarized police force which possesses the capacity to effectively shield government from the people, immunizing government from the accountability to which it is otherwise susceptible where the public retains the means to carry it out: the means to practically petition for a redress of grievances or to practically gauge the 'consent of the governed' which is said to form the basis of 'just government'.

Or consider the baseless enforcement of various policies (and political precedents established) pertaining to masking and 'social distancing' during the lockdowns beginning in 2020; policies, not *legitimate laws*, enforced and embraced even by members of the citizenry who've bought into them, who contact the 'authorities' to bring violence (and financial consequences) upon their neighbors who are out of compliance; policies restricting people's freedom to travel, their freedom to assemble, their freedom to worship and practice their religions, their freedom to host social gatherings on their own private property; policies threatening and intimidating the public; policies arousing fear and subjecting the people to the coerced administration of experimental mRNA 'vaccines'; policies suffered by the people for such sinful desires as seeking to freely travel or go shopping, to keep their conditions of employment, to protect their dignity and their medical freedom, to continue operating their businesses, to celebrate occasions with friends and family, to witness the birth of a newborn or to accompany a loved one who is dying or in ill-health, to arrange for proper funerals and burials for loved ones, to honor the precious customs and traditions of those committed to culture or faith, or to simply preserve some semblance of humanity during the COVID-19 pandemic. None too surprising, the members of the state (and the greater establishment) during this time were not only hidden behind their desks, on leave or 'working from home', but concealed conveniently behind their masks and served just as conveniently by their conscience and their peace of mind (in the form of job security) as by their claims on 'the science' and 'the law', the latter having little to no basis in the former.

Ultimately, the essential safeguards of freedom are maintained through the capacity of the individual to secure his freedom for himself, to be secure, by natural right, in his person, property, and effects. Where government boasts of its 'generosity' in its allowance of movement, personal choice, or any genuinely 'peaceful protest', it is an admission of its instinct to thwart it. As evidenced by the intimidating presence and 'qualified immunity' of police officers across modern America, a government too insulated from the people will invariably own them.

These are not rare events in America but part of daily life in that country where the people have long ago abandoned the uniquely American traditions of skepticism and eternal vigilance toward the abuses of government. Indeed, these kinds of events are even expected in any other country of the world which more readily acknowledges its police state. However, Americans are rather unique in the way that their traditions of bygone eras keep them in denial: the noble ideas and traditions of an America free and independent, visions of *the land of the free and the home of the brave*, the portraits of free and rugged pioneers standing tall and alone on the prairie, the spirit of '76 and that of the American who still fancies himself part of that lost tradition and that largely-forgotten cause.

What's more, it is not an epidemic unique to any particular race or ethnicity, not an abuse of power selectively sparing others among the public; it is a case of equal opportunity abuse stemming from a rampant culture problem across (federal, state, and local) police departments in America, not at all separate from the training, hiring practices, general attitudes, and known mental illnesses so common within departments — a problem exacerbated by mobbing, complacency, and negative experiences, ultimately fostering a deep-seated resentment for the public they are charged to "protect and serve".

Hereafter, I offer an account of one of my own personal encounters with *law enforcement* and the so-called 'justice system'. The following testimony offers insight into the events of my 2014 arrest. As will be shown, the officers involved in the events violated not only the indispensable principle of self-ownership but the supreme law of the land: the Constitution of the United States.

In this testimony, I spare no detail to expose the absurdity of the business of government, which is to squash its benefactors under the thumb of 'official business', to forcibly expand upon the people's obligations to, and yet their overall dependence upon, the system which asserts its authority over them. The people predictably yield where they have been so thoroughly groomed to adhere to the norms, to respect 'authority' as a means to survival, 'success', and acceptance, to view the establishment as having its place and remaining worthy of the people's embrace; yielding as they accept the stated intentions or 'justifications' of those who abuse their 'authority', where the people either acquiesce or, through their shortsightedness of judgment, their ignorance of the philosophical, the economic, and the political, come to accept that which is seen (or promised) at the expense of that which is unseen (or likely to happen as a result).

In the end, the result is a sacrifice of some measure of freedom for some measure (or promise) of *security*, but all that this consistently manages to accomplish is to replace the threats against liberty, real or imaginary, with the constant threats of intransigent institutions defended by well-armed men and women adorned with badges and the benefit of conscience, who view the public, almost indiscriminately and without exception, as common criminals or criminals-in-the-making.

MY TESTIMONY
BY J. M. ROCK

On the afternoon of July 28th, 2014, I was driving home in my 1996 Oldsmobile Cutlass. I had just purchased a week of groceries at the local Kroger, and I was looking forward to getting home so I could enjoy some of the Breyer's ice cream I had just purchased. However, this was not to be.

Contrary to the vision I had of returning home to have some ice cream after work, looking forward to the peace and comfort of my apartment after the two-minute drive from the grocery store, I would instead be met by flashing lights and flashy badges. Not least of all, I would eventually return home hours later with a head injury, badly-bruised limbs, and a carton of melted ice cream reminding me of the expired promise of a pleasant afternoon.

The following text documents the unfortunate events of that afternoon. This testimony was written on the twenty-ninth of July, 2014, then later typed, edited, and slightly revised for the benefit of readability. I trust that these details, in their honest and accurate portrayal of events, will provide the reader with particular evidence of the kinds of qualities that have come to define 'professional law enforcement' across the United States. Through my testimony, the torture of Bobby Fischer in the Pasadena Jailhouse, the sieges at Waco and Ruby Ridge, and the killing of Tony Timpa, we have but a few poignant examples of some of the abuses committed, some more commonly than others, by 'law enforcement' in the name of 'justice' and 'official business'. My hope is that my testimony and the others will remind readers of the sacred cause we've inherited from our forebears: the responsibility of defending our heirs from such abuses of power so that they themselves may know peace and freedom, that they themselves may be spared the indignities attending too little of either, and that they themselves will honor the price paid by those who knew personally what was at stake.

MY TESTIMONY

My First and Fourth Amendment rights, among others, including those enumerated under *Title 18 U.S. Code Chapter 13, Section 241*, were violated on the afternoon of July 28th, 2014. I was arrested after briefly honking my horn near a police scene — an attempt to warn approaching vehicles and incoming traffic of my presence, an action I deemed necessary due to the precarious positioning of the police cars obscuring the view around the bend of the road.

Upon suddenly noticing flashing lights behind me in my rearview mirror, I immediately pulled into a parking spot in The Village apartment complex, where I currently reside. When Novi Police Officer Sergeant Warren arrived at my window, I asked for his reason for pulling me over. He acknowledged me and demanded that I wait while he presumably documented and reported my license plate number.

The officer, whom I then and again later identified as Sergeant Warren (badge number: 219), then approached my window, which was entirely rolled down so as to permit an easy and free exchange of words and documentation. After asking the officer to explain the purpose of the stop, I immediately presented my license but hesitated to hand it over to the officer, who shortly thereafter summoned backup before proceeding to demand that I relinquish possession of my license, registration, and proof of insurance.

I identified myself as the owner and operator of the vehicle and notified the officer that I would provide him with registration and proof of insurance, but that I only first ask that he detail the reason for the stop along with the reasonable suspicion upon which the stop was based. I asked him to describe the crime that I had committed, or the crime that I had been suspected of committing. But again, I received no answer to these questions.

Upon the arrival of two other officers at the scene, I begged each of the officers to explain the reason for the stop. Apparently, all of the officers on scene had only one intention: to force my compliance with their arbitrary demands, inspired presumably by frustration with a citizen exercising his rights or by their loose interpretation of some equivocal and equally unreasonable set of laws which any man could, without any evidence and at any time, be suspected of committing, whether it be 'disorderly conduct', 'resisting arrest', 'contempt of cop', or, more specifically, angering an officer by honking a car horn.

In short, as was the dialogue between the four of us, the officers displayed no intention of allowing me to speak or to understand the cause of my detention and eventual arrest. The three officers, at the behest of Sergeant Warren, began to impatiently and forcibly remove me from my vehicle. Unfortunately, my window had been rolled down, which — conveniently for them — permitted easy access to my driver-side door lock. Sergeant Warren then unlocked my car door, violently flung the door open, then grabbed me by my arms to drag me from my car — during which time I had remained buckled into my seat.

After I had finally released the buckle, the three officers grabbed and threw me to the ground, aggressively pinning my legs and smashing my head against the pavement. I repeatedly expressed that I was not resisting and that I would comply. All attempts were in vain, however, for the officers were obviously hellbent on exercising their brute force over me, which, as it turns out, they knew all along would go unchecked by any measure of accountability or any semblance of justice in front of a judge already infamous for corruption.

While dragging me from my car and hurling me to the ground, the officers commanded me to stop resisting, all while I had acted much like a noodle, attempting no resistance at all. The officers threatened to use their tasers while continuing to throw me around and abuse my limbs. I had on countless occasions begged them to ease their force and to permit my compliance. No such leniency was granted. I wanted nothing more than to end this torture in order to return to my residence to unload my groceries and relax after a day of work. After they attached their cuffs to my wrists, the officers rushed me to a patrol car and forced me into the backseat, manhandling me the entire way.

From there, I watched the officers enter my vehicle to proceed with a 'search', which really amounted to them making a mess of everything in my center console, my glove compartment, and the groceries in my backseat. I had nothing to hide in my car (not that it should matter), but I was quite disturbed by this process and their mistreatment of me and my personal property, and I was particularly disturbed for I had never consented to a search, and I was still unclear as to the charges leveled against me.

During the search, one of the officers approached me to insist that I comply in order to make things easier, with an attitude indicating frustration with (possibly) a hint of guilt and sympathy for my poor treatment — yet this was a bit unusual, as I believed that I had already made abundantly clear my readiness to comply. After minutes of a hasty yet thorough search, the officers departed from my vehicle, slamming the doors and leaving the interior in complete disarray. At this time Sergeant Warren returned to his squad car to escort me to the station for booking and fingerprints. At the station, I continued to comply with Sergeant Warren and the two cadets on duty: Cadet Mitchell and his senior cadet in command.

The two cadets processed my booking information along with my fingerprints, following a thorough pat-down by Sergeant Warren. Following the booking procedure, I posted bond in the amount of $100 cash, whereafter I was escorted to a lobby in the building to pay a $20 cash fee for my vehicle release. Cadet Mitchell executed this transaction under the supervision of his fellow senior-ranking cadet. Shortly thereafter, I set out by foot to find Hadley's Towing, where my car had been impounded — this despite the fact that I had pled with the officers to leave my car where it was parked, in my parking spot in front of my apartment. Despite this, the officers insisted, over my reluctance, that my vehicle be towed. Upon arriving at Hadley's Towing, I was charged an additional $85 in cash for the release of my vehicle from the lot. In the end, I had incurred $205 of fees and a loss of more than 3 hours of my life, not an insignificant sum.

That moment was one in which I take no pride and which I entirely regret. I know that each of us involved in the events outlined herein can learn a number of lessons from this incident, and I truly hope that this opportunity is seized. I take full responsibility for my actions, and I have certainly learned a great deal from this incident. Let it be known, however, that I had on that day no intentions of disobeying orders. I had no intentions of creating a scene or causing a disturbance. I only wished to be secure in my property and my personal effects, and to defend my personal rights as a free and independent human being, and as an American.

As a result of the arrest, the lengthy booking process, posting bond, paying to have the police department release my vehicle from the impound lot, paying the towing company and the later court costs, I had been fined more than $1,200 in fees, I had sustained significant bodily injury, I had been convicted of a misdemeanor, and I had lost over six hours of my life as a free and independent man; the latter of those losses being the most unforgivable aspect of the whole incident.

With this written account, I submit my plea for justice, not only in my case but to prevent further abuses of power. While I would like to request compensation at least for my financial losses, I more urgently plead for justice in the form of accountability, in the form of a message sent to officers here and elsewhere that this kind of treatment is unacceptable and cannot, and will not, be tolerated in a society which proudly places a value on such concepts as *liberty* and *justice;* that this type of behavior will never be tolerated and that my children, all of our children, will never suffer the indignities of a society tolerant of abuse.

THE FRATERNAL ORDER OF PAWNS

BY J. M. ROCK

In an altercation captured through Facebook Live on January 16, 2018, political activist and libertarian presidential candidate Adam Kokesh was detained by highway patrol while traveling in his RV across the state of Texas.

While detained near the city of Decatur, part of the Dallas-Fort Worth metroplex, Kokesh admirably attempted to reason with the arresting officer after he was apparently stopped for exceeding the speed limit, attaining a speed of 74 miles per hour in a reported 65 MPH zone.

After a discouraging exchange with the officer, a number of backup officers arrived on the scene. By all accounts, the event appeared under control while Kokesh remained calm, composed and cooperative during the entire process.

After the original officer momentarily returned to his squad car, Kokesh initiated a discussion with the other two responding officers who had arrived as backup. During this exchange, Kokesh introduced the officers to his book *FREEDOM!*, urging them to recall the principles that had guided them to the profession, which had presumably inspired them toward public service in the first place; the principles enshrined in the oath they've sworn to uphold.

As Kokesh then pointed out, many of those reasons and many of those causes are under threat by the actual operations of government; the officers' actions included (where they sought to 'justify' a vehicle search on a stop pertaining to speeding), and by the policymaking of politicians who determine the kinds of 'justice' served, who arbitrarily define terms like 'criminal' and 'suspicion' to their liking, and who determine the kinds of agendas promoted by police officers through selective enforcement; with the members of law enforcement, of course, purporting to represent the interests of their communities while in practice primarily serving the interests of self-serving bureaucrats, prosecutors and politicians.

During this interaction, Kokesh seemed to have reached the officers on a personal level, even appearing to have evoked smiles and excitement from his police audience. However, he pointed out the fact that the bureaucracy is always putting obstacles between cop and 'civilian', that there is always that discomfort between the anxious citizen and the threatening, intimidating officer; that instead of two citizens having a cordial conversation, "it's a real shame that we have government in between us," that we would otherwise have "people being able to interact without a coercive monopoly interfering with those relationships."

Kokesh also elaborated on one of the fundamental contradictions expressed by the first officer, who asked Kokesh whether he would prefer that a criminal be apprehended and thoroughly vetted or permitted to travel freely until the next stop.

Kokesh explained that the nature of the stop and the legitimacy of the law are of specific importance here, reminding the officer of these basic truths: that not all laws are just, not all laws are legitimate, and not all laws are correctly understood or properly enforced by those sworn to serve. Specifically, Kokesh pointed out: "If the 'criminal' has got a busted taillight or an expired registration, no, I don't want that person stopped. I want them to be able to take care of that as easily as possible; and in that sense we have the government, the politicians, deciding who's a criminal and who's not, and you guys have to go out and enforce the law, even if it's unjust, and I think that's a real travesty, that's a real source of injustice."

Kokesh continued by saying, "I think a lot of the tensions between police and the communities where they work is because they're not serving the communities first. They have to serve their boss first, and they have to serve the politicians, and they have to serve government first, and obviously the government doesn't represent the will of the people, by any stretch of the imagination."

Beyond these, such sins as "busted taillights" and "expired registrations", and the long list of petty infractions that each of us is likely violating at any given moment (due purely to the ever wider scope and equivocal language of *laws* and *regulations*), the more nuanced yet most significant aspect of this story, and others like it, is found in the kinds of policing and politicking which have, in practice, combined to distort the relationships, the interactions and the power dynamics between public servants and the public they have vowed to serve.

As for the members of law enforcement relative to each individual citizen, the officers' obligations to the public increase in proportion with the powers and technologies afforded them; the influence of an increasingly powerful and militarized police force introducing roles and responsibilities which require of each officer an ever higher level of discipline and proper discretion, the kinds of discipline demanding of the officer a certain sobriety and certainty of mind, a certain measure of conviction in distinguishing legitimate laws from those which are illegitimate, in constantly comparing his actions to the ideal standards of those laws and his own virtues, and in prioritizing those virtues and laws (while contesting misconduct and refusing to enforce illegitimate ones) over the security of his own job.

Most law enforcement officers, however, prioritize the latter, seeking to guarantee comfortable lives for themselves and, among those who have them, their own families; this being understandable and relatable but strictly incompatible with the unique requirements of the job, especially a job well done.

In this sense, their ideological inconsistencies, wherever they maintain any personal convictions or meaningful thoughts of their own, represent a culture of conflicting priorities: a culture based on following orders, backing up the administration and their fellow cops without question and at all times, and doing whatever they imagine will earn praise or draw less flak from leadership.

So the position of a law enforcement officer is often an unprincipled one where such things as philosophical curiosity, thinking for oneself, and even taking the oath seriously, are considered dangerous, even redundant, in that environment in which the law's interpretation is assumed the sole responsibility of judges, the ones officially appointed to do the real thinking, the ones assumed the vendors of justice.

And for those who eventually see the injustice for what it is, the pensions, the benefits and the job security are just too tempting, while the bureaucratic challenges faced by doing the right thing are, apparently, often too much and often coming at too high of a price to warrant the risk of standing on principle. That is precisely why the individual, the one witnessing or aware of officers in the act of committing any injustice, are called to exert 'external control' on government; those encountering officers in the act often being the very victims of such abuse, the very ones being accosted and apprehended.

Unfortunately, as the 'Father of the Constitution' James Madison proclaimed in *Federalist No. 51*, we are imperfect and we are mortal: "If angels were to govern men, neither external nor internal controls on government would be necessary."

Those controls are maintained only through the forces of eternal vigilance and citizen participation, the kinds maintaining a healthy skepticism toward the institutions possessing unimaginable power, capable of unfathomable destruction. And where the controls have been so heavily manipulated to favor government to such an extent that so many stand to lose so much by standing against it, that is the end of free thinking and the end of a free society; this is a society desperate for revolution.

Part and parcel of the modern American experience has been the incredible incompetence of public service, over time becoming a field dominated progressively by more and more 'professionals' distinguished mostly by their remarkable mediocrity, their distinct inability to do much else, and their attitudes of hostility or indifference toward the public; each individual of the public being regarded as a criminal or a nuisance at best. All the while, these 'public servants' are vested with the kinds of authority and treated to the kinds of salaries and benefits wildly out of proportion with the quality and trustworthiness of their work, the value of which remains unknown while the costs of which continue going up. While they might view themselves as 'professionals', they are more properly compared to sloths, just as they are in the 2016 animated comedy *Zootopia*. But don't allow that comparison to let your guard down, to make you think that these particular 'sloths', the ones in government, are in any sense cute, cuddly or nonthreatening. This particular type of 'sloth' has just enough energy and just enough power to make your life miserable.

Compared to the sloth of 'public service' we have the cheetahs and the mules of free enterprise, the workers carrying the weight, the investors carrying the risk, and the innovators eager to resolve real-world problems. The brilliance of free enterprise is in its foundation in time-tested first principles, its accountability in real time, its ability to identify and resolve problems through a decentralized network of individual actors free in their own right. One beautiful aspect of this system is that the 'authority' of any man relative to another is determined by the terms of their own contracts. Additionally, any failures in such a system are owned by the individuals responsible and the institutions they represent.

So, on the whole, whereas in a free market the failures of business can (and indeed tend to) be addressed with tweaks and innovations, the replacement of administrations, the shifting of capital away from inefficient ends, and the implementation of fresh ideas and improved systems, the sloths in government seldom learn, seldom have impetus or occasion to 'improve', whatever that could possibly mean for some of the 'work' they claim to do. Indeed, the sloths in government carry on across generations with mere changing of the guard, with each failure 'justifying' more power to the state, more animosity toward the public and more sluggish attitudes toward the kinds of 'work' already expected to be slow and inefficient; their 'work' behind badges and banners inherited along with the tolerance of a people who view that kind of 'work' as part of life, whereas many of their ancestors had rightly viewed it with ridicule or skepticism.

However, time seems to pass in the blink of an eye and the skeptics themselves pass in due time, leaving the absurd and the unreasonable of their days representing the possibilities and potential norms for the future, a future approaching much faster than sensed or believed, and a future that ultimately isn't even theirs, a future the skeptics would hardly recognize if they hadn't adapted along the way; with skepticism towards the 'absurd' and the 'unreasonable' yielding in short order to collective acceptance or embrace, the once-initiated men passing the torch to unhardened boys who inherit those customs as 'institutions' and 'traditions', assuming them tolerable for the fact that their predecessors managed to live with them and leave them to their heirs.

Endeavoring ever further into the absurd, appearances remain much the same, at least on the surface; changes subtle enough to avoid detection, to limit any commotion. With the people adapting to their environments, the badges as shiny as ever, the police more proud, more arrogant and all the more powerful, they forget the doubts and uncertainties, the skepticism and apprehensions of prior generations, those of the people who ceded the power with specific intent and those of the officers once cautious eventually policing with contempt.

The primary difference between these generations is not insignificant: whereas the boys of old at least had some doubts, the boys of today do without them, going about their 'official business' with the full benefit and backing of cemented 'traditions', with the full complement of legal protections and high-tech munitions; an arsenal at their disposal and thus encouraging their use.

As it turns out, while some might claim an interest in 'serving their community', most police candidates pursue careers in law enforcement for a short list of reasons: for status, job security and benefits unavailable to them elsewhere; out of desperation, privately acknowledging their own deficiencies in intellect or creativity; or for the concept of public service, that concept carrying less weight and failing the people over time.

The career of the law enforcement officer, even most of his daily life, is driven by the idea that he knows best, that he should force other people to live in accordance with the way he believes others ought to live, or at least in accordance with the ideas he's been trained to accept; the very thing, 'life' itself, representing the average officer's greatest failure, and, when considering the form it takes in others, the most repugnant of things imaginable.

Indeed, these beliefs form the basis of the officer's behavior not just in the course of his 'duties' but in his own personal life, where he is just as aggressive with the people who cross him, who challenge him, or who plain frustrate and annoy him.

In fact, a wide variety of research shows that the incidence of household and family violence is at least two to four times higher in the law-enforcement community than in the general population; that, according to one particular source, police have a much bigger domestic-abuse problem than the National Football League (NFL) does. Of course, the incidence of violence in the homes of police officers is naturally underreported, given the fact that, in these cases, the offenders work within the institutions responsible for conducting the investigations, and their colleagues, who themselves are violent in their own households and can therefore relate, are nearly always willing to turn the other way or let their buddies off the hook.

Now, the causal relationship between law enforcement and household abuse (and police brutality in general) can likely be reduced to a rather short list of explanations:

1. Those who join the ranks of law enforcement tend to have short tempers and distinct propensities toward violence as a means to conflict resolution; even demonstrated by their mere interest in carrying out such work. The 'work' itself tends to reinforce and exacerbate these behaviors.

2. Veterans of law enforcement have experience with all kinds of people, but generally they deal with people at their worst, who are having a bad day, or who have their own temperament issues; temperaments often exacerbated by the fact that officers aren't in control of their *own* emotions, largely due to the fact that fellow officers are nearly always willing to back them up (and therefore officers tend to think they're doing the right thing). Officers contend with all sorts of conditions and crime scenes, witnessing death and disfigurement

and facing physical threats, crises, and urgent situations on a regular basis in the course of their careers. This leads to conditions conducive to the development of post-traumatic stress disorder (PTSD), a mental and behavioral disorder not yet taken very seriously among officers who view treatment as a sign of weakness, or who are otherwise ignorant to the condition, given the fact that they surround themselves almost exclusively with fellow officers; or considering the fact that so many are out of touch with their own thoughts and feelings, lacking control over and insight into their emotions, or simply in denial about the possibility of having a disorder, so many cops being narcissists and sociopaths who wouldn't dare admit that possibility (or being too arrogant to consider it). In fact, a variety of studies show that as much as one-third of active law enforcement officers exhibit some form of PTSD; another statistic potentially understating the truth, given the aforementioned stigma around seeking treatment and, it is worth noting, the propensity of cops to be dishonest with themselves and others.

3. The bureaucracy, the training, and the demands of the position condition law enforcement officers to assume attitudes of righteousness, to disregard the plights and rights of others, to intimidate, manipulate and gaslight as means to managing or controlling situations, to lie

and cheat to gain an advantage or to protect themselves (and fellow officers) from consequences attending their actions, as evidenced in one particular context by the National Center for Women and Policing: "Even officers who are found guilty of domestic violence are unlikely to be fired, arrested, or referred for prosecution."

Unfortunately, the bulk of the evidence here creates the profile of individuals with ambitions exceeding their ability to accomplish much of anything through nonviolent means.

If they cannot achieve their ends through patient deliberation or thoughtful discussion, for which the vast majority of them have neither the appetite nor the tolerance, they can triumph only through force or intimidation.

As one of the officers candidly admitted in his discussion with Adam Kokesh, he became a law enforcement officer because he "doesn't like the way people drive."

The other officer didn't even have an answer to that basic question, an answer that any 'public servant' should be able to deliver to any member of the public on a moment's notice.

In fact, this is famously known in sales parlance as the *elevator pitch*; and if any 'professional' is unable to describe the nature of or motivation behind his work in that span of time, it's likely that he's either not passionate about the work or not qualified to do it.

In summary, the majority of the law-enforcement community is comprised of disappointments who never quite realized their potential and others who settled into the career field as a way to enhance their social status, to bully or to wield authority over others, or to simply enjoy the financial benefits of a stable job and the guarantee of a pension (and health insurance) in retirement.

Most who become law enforcement officers do so in an effort to salvage a life, and perhaps a legacy or some self-respect, that would be better served by some serious introspection and a dose of humility before exploiting a career, a badge and a gun to imperil the freedoms of their fellow man, all in order to continue the charade of pretending to be something more than they are; all in order to convince themselves, as well as others, that this is true.

Unfortunately, government has made it all too profitable to ignore principle in favor of institutionalized force and coercion.

For this reason, law enforcement officers are known to evade debate, or to otherwise prematurely shut it down, by declaring, "I'm not going to argue with you," or by physically punctuating the event with a punch, a takedown, or an arrest.

Whether due to intellectual incompetence or a stubborn unwillingness to participate in conversation with the public, the outcome is the same: an empowered yet ill-guided male-factor employing his favorite tool, violence or the threat thereof, to force his subject to submit to his control.

In the case of Adam Kokesh's arrest on January 16, 2018, where he was eventually booked on *suspicion* of contraband (after a drug dog 'alerted' to the possible presence of drugs), it appears that this has been just another episode of the same systemic misconduct that we've grown to expect from the robotic and hypocritical agents at the helm of the unrelenting machine bulldozing the public; a public apparently accustomed to the abuse and generally willing to take it.

Too many tyrants across history have been celebrated, even mythologized, through comics, motion pictures and heroic caricatures for mankind to have even the slimmest chance of surmounting the deep social and psychological conditioning which has accompanied the growing delusion; it will require nothing short of a great awakening and a willing people to shake off these chains.

The police state is here, ladies and gentlemen, and it dominates our roads, our commercial activities, our personal and domestic lives more intimately and more broadly than ever, and more so than one can possibly appreciate. As Kokesh puts it, "The greatest enemies of the Constitution are not to be found in the sands of some far-off land but rather right here at home."

We can either defend the Constitution, defend our freedom and our inalienable rights, by contesting every margin and letting the tyrants know exactly what they're up against, or we can surrender incrementally, inch by inch until they have trampled every mile of our freedoms as individuals, extinguishing the light from the shining city upon the hill, the final flame of hope, reason and enlightenment flickering in the eye of a violent storm threatening to put it out.

It's up to you.

DIGNITY BE DAMNED

by J. M. ROCK

As for the growing irreverence toward the precious institution of private property, it threatens the essential foundation for heritage, legacy and self-purpose; as for the bigger picture, the right to and respect for private property preserves the sovereignty of the individual, the dignity of man and family, and their security in their affairs, their effects, and in their person, and ultimately it represents the essential condition to their liberty, their individuality, and their self-defense. That loss of respect, even that growing disdain, toward private property is yet another instance of the growing desensitization to the master-slave relationship, in the era of soft despotism and intellectual excuses aiming to 'justify' theft, *dignity be damned*; these being the markers down the road to serfdom.

Indeed, a whole variety of myths and misconceptions have arisen out of the comforts, conveniences, and artifices of the modern world. As the world develops economically

and technologically, as it proceeds with the illusions maintained politically, it appears that the people grow just as dis-
tant to the throes of reality, stuck ever more in the abstract
and the virtual away from the tangible and the terrestrial.
In just this way, the people have begun to develop new
ways of thinking about the world and each other, and they
and their followers have come to fancy themselves more
'progressive' for matching their pitch. Whether it's mis-
placed faith in cryptocurrency or democracy, or whether
it's the perennial alarmism around such politically-motived
theories as manmade climate change, the modern world is
rife with myths and misconceptions. Another prime example which affects us all is the belief that everything can
be replaced, that there is nothing worth defending with
physical or lethal force or our lives: as one self-described
expert on YouTube puts it, "We shouldn't use deadly force
to protect our property."

Now, it's worth noting that the so-called expert isn't
alone here. He has a lot of company. Some of his support-
ers have claimed that burglars shouldn't be met with force
or violence if they haven't presented the same. One such
supporter put it this way: "I'm only saying that your will-
ingness to kill or injure [someone] over losing [sic] property without danger to life or limb is equally wrong, and
two wrongs don't make a right." Another such supporter
has asked rhetorically, "You don't shoot people for keying

your car, breaking a contract, or TP-ing your house, would you? Even though all of those things cost you money and time? Why is that?" While these incredulous types aren't generally interested in answers, we will explore them here.

As we begin, let's address the first of those two quotes: the claim that it is equally wrong to kill or injure a burglar. Before continuing, it's worth noting that the commenter phrased his statement quite differently than I have just transcribed it. I dare say that this was intentional, as it accords with the character profile to be explored later in the reading. Instead of attributing the act to the burglar, he opted instead to equivocate both the identity and the crime. In this case, the victim isn't merely threatening to "kill or injure [someone] over losing [sic] property"; indeed, the truth is that, in presenting potentially lethal force or with the criminal knowing to expect it, the victim (or the potential target) stands to defend his rightful property by using sufficient means to deter or prevent a criminal from stealing his property and doing any further damage; notice that this is a form of deterring, preventing, or responding to an action of 'stealing', an act of theft, not a condition of merely 'losing property'. This is the modifying distinction between the home invasion and the acts of keying a car, breaking a contract, or TP-ing a house: the former comes with a reasonable risk of further damage, up to and including bodily harm and death to the homeowners. In the case of a home invasion, there is nowhere to safely retreat, and there is no reason to assume that a home invader will suddenly become reasonable.

Now, another commenter claims, "burglary is specifically theft without threat of violence." Bearing this in mind, I've taken the time to consult a variety of sources to accurately present the common and legal definitions of burglary. Here is what I've found:

TheFreeDictionary.com defines burglary as "trespassory breaking and entering of the dwelling of another with an intent to commit a felony therein. It is an offense against possession and habitation."

According to LegalDictionary.net, "Burglary is a crime defined as unlawful entry into a building or structure with the intent to commit a crime." An alternate definition describes burglary as "Entry into a building or structure without permission from the owner with the intent to commit a crime."

The Merriam-Webster dictionary defines burglary as "the act of breaking and entering a dwelling to commit a felony (such as theft)."

Finally, the Cambridge Dictionary defines burglary as "the crime of illegally entering a building and stealing things."

According to these definitions, burglary is not a crime lacking the threat of violence. In fact, TheFreeDictionary.com describes it as "breaking and entering" and "an offense against possession and habitation." Surely, against any reasonable standard, "breaking and entering" and "an offense against possession and habitation" would qualify as an implied or even explicit threat of violence. The common thread between these four sources is that burglary, at minimum, implies unlawful entry and theft. Now, I would argue that it's not all that important to determine or operate from this definition, but TheFreeDictionary.com does well to identify an important feature of burglary: the "offense against... habitation."

This is actually far more important than it might appear, as it indicates that burglary is not just a threat posed to property, but rather a threat to the whole residence. As explained previously, there is a meaningful difference between burglary and the acts of "keying a car, breaking a contract, or TP-ing a house." One of those differences is that, in the estimation of any reasonable person, a burglar presents a potential risk of death or bodily harm to the victims. After all, the victims don't know at the time of the crime whether he's just a plain burglar or the murdering kind. In any event, wherever a criminal has presented an "offense against... habitation", it is safe to assume that he doesn't respect you or your rights. Whether a plain burglar or the murdering kind, it's not a question of whether he threatens your life, your liberty, or your property; it's a question of only how much of it he'll take.

Now, having already justified potentially-lethal force in the defense of life, liberty, and property, let's proceed to debunk the myth that "all things can be replaced." Let's begin by pointing out the obvious: not all things can be replaced. The claim that "all things can be replaced" is not just overly simplistic but potentially dangerous, as it threatens the very nature and the very product of life on our planet.

Not everything in life is fungible or replaceable; not everything in life has a market value, or one commensurate with the value the victim might place on it; the significance of such objects as heirlooms, artifacts, and prized possessions carrying a sentimental and deeply-personal value beyond measure. There are many things in life that are unique, that have sentimental or spiritual value, that are worth more to their owners than they are in their appraisal. Above all, there are many things and prized possessions that are priceless, or that otherwise come to inspire, to represent a legacy, or to define life. For example, in some aboriginal cultures, the people prize their collection of their ancestors' remains. For them, this is a time-honored tradition and a way to pay tribute to their forbears. In still other cases, people collect artifacts and heirlooms passed down through generations. This is how they preserve and honor their memory. In this particular case, it is obvious that theft would leave the family without any recourse at all if the property went unrecovered. Even if it were eventually recovered, there is no way to recover the loss and the indignity suffered by the family. After all, no society can be said to value life, liberty, or property which doesn't value all three.

The problem with the modern Western world is that most of its inhabitants don't distinguish between *price* and *value*, and for this reason they don't appreciate the true value of life and an honest day's work, the true value of freedom, liberty and personal sovereignty; it is for just this reason that they don't appreciate the legacy and heritage they've inherited or, in time, the ones they stand to leave behind. Where they view the world, its contents, and each other through the lens of commerce, they regard them as replaceable commodities not worth defending; in fact, as far as they're concerned, the only things worth defending are those of specific sociopolitical value, or those things that are important to *them*.

Of course, this is the easiest position to defend, because a stern debate is their only challenge. They betray their intuition and their instincts in favor of abstract intellectualisms, which they claim to accept out of moral obligation, but which they accept only out of convenience. These intellectualisms have ultimately come to replace their family values and time-tested traditions; above all, they've come to loosen their grip on reality and to warp their sense of *right* and *wrong*. Of course, this doesn't keep them from being clever.

In fact, upon the abandonment of principle, anything goes. In their view, for example, they claim that it's wrong to wield potentially-lethal force against someone who's threatening or stealing private property. Ironically, their argument doesn't even stand on its own. When questioned, they'll even resort to using the victims' own last resort against them: the victims' own private insurance. They'll claim, "This is why people have insurance." Of course, they pay no mind to the fact that people have fire insurance not so that arsonists can burn their houses down, but so that they're protected in the event of an unforeseen accident. They pay no mind to the fact that people have health insurance not so that assailants can harm them, but so that their health and wellbeing can be restored after an unexpected accident. They pay no mind to the fact that people have life insurance not so that murderers can kill them, but so that their respective families are financially protected against that loss.

They fail to recognize that insurance does not cover the total loss; it covers merely part of the financial ramifications. They fail to accept that insurance serves to protect people financially against part of the loss associated with an accident or unexpected event; it does not serve to strip people of their responsibility, or to act as a substitute for morality. As stated previously, these people don't distinguish between *price* and *value*, so, as they prefer to see it, whether it's a loss of property or a loss of life, it can all be replaced in kind or in cash. If only the perpetrators carried their own liability insurance, then apparently, as the useful idiots see it, there'd be no need for any moral standard at all. Granted, this is precisely their proposed antidote for every social problem: systems over people.

One of those systems, in this case, seeks to defend the criminals. Make no mistake, this isn't because they deserve it. First, it's worth noting that there is a difference between rights and political protections. In this case, no criminal has the right to threaten another's life or property. While statutes may stand to defend the criminal in some cases, they are not in place to declare his rights, nor to distinguish between *right* and *wrong*; in most cases those protections exist as the consequence of ambiguity, a technicality or, otherwise, a narrow-minded prosecutor or political cause.

Most reasonable people would agree that a slave has a right to threaten or even use violence to gain his freedom. There is hardly a difference between a slave holder and a burglar: both seek to exploit the other's life and labor for his own benefit; however, the burglar doesn't want any of the former's added responsibility. Of course, that comes as no surprise, given that responsible people don't steal or invade other people's homes.

In this comparison, it is the slave holder who is the more ethical of the two, as he operates from no false pretense. After all, the slave at least knows his place, his purpose, and the form and function of his labor; and he at least knows his master and has some kind of working relationship with him. The slave holder even allows the slave to enjoy some (or even most) of the fruits of his own labor; and, in many cases, he provides the slave shelter and invests in his health and welfare; and in still others cases he grants the slave the opportunity to pay his way to freedom.

Meanwhile the burglar does nothing more than to exploit the life and labor of his victim, to threaten his victim with force to get what he wants, and to enjoy the fruits and the protections of a feckless and senseless bureaucracy; a bureaucracy particularly lax on crime (and complicit itself) and, for reasons related to fear or politics, failing to perform the duties they are hired to perform. As for that comparison to the slave holder, the burglar does absolutely nothing in return. Instead, the burglar exploits and threatens his victim's home, his private property, his labor, and his very life. The burglar is a slave holder, except that he takes from the unsuspecting, he exploits the faults and failings of a feckless bureaucracy, and he returns nothing to the people whom he exploits for his own benefit. In just this way, the burglar isn't just a slave holder; he's a criminal who places precious little value on life, liberty and property, and yet there's a whole bureaucracy and an entire cohort of people who seek to defend him.

Ultimately, wherever any person is under threat, coercion or intimidation to forfeit any of his property, or wherever any person has trespassed to effect the same, the victim is held as a slave to the whims and wants of the assailant, held indefinitely at his mercy. The primary difference between the acts themselves is that it's not very difficult to visualize slaves being held to labor against their will, while it's more challenging (and abstract) when accounting for the labor that's already been done. Whether a person is held to labor today or whether he's made to forfeit his labor from yesterday, the consequence is all the same.

Ultimately, every living and breathing person on this planet has the right to defend his property in the event that intentional destruction or theft of property is imminent; or intentional trespass or destruction imminently poses a threat of injury or death. This right is ironclad.

While there are some institutions around the world that have encroached upon this right, that are ignorant enough to contest it, there are many others that have expressly preserved it. Remember, rights are not given to us by men, but inherited naturally from our Creator; they can merely be protected by men and the statutes they enact. There is no moral or ethical argument to refute this, nor any words in any language that can possibly be strung together to justify the suspension of these rights.

The principal moral imperative in all of the world is the non-aggression principle, which forbids the initiation of force or fraud. As property is an extension of the person and the product of his labor, any intentional force or fraud directed at person or property is immoral. The defender is therefore well within his rights to defend his property and his person, to defend his family and his home, by protest or by force, by all means practicable and reasonable, to the extent that the threat is neutralized and no longer present, that the perpetrator is restrained and to be formally held to account for his transgressions.

Just as no person ought ever to be held to labor against his will, and just as no one ought to be unjustly deprived of his rights or the protections upon them, no person ought ever to be stripped of his right to defend his life, liberty, and property; no person ought ever to face this or any other unsolicited torture, especially at the hands or through the complicity of the bureaucracy charged with defending those rights. Wherever we ignore or minimize the absolute right to defend either of those three, we stand to diminish them all in time.

I WAS TORTURED
IN THE PASADENA JAILHOUSE
BY BOBBY FISCHER

Bank Robbery...

About 2:00 p.m. Tuesday afternoon, May 26, 1981, as I was peacefully and lawfully walking towards Lake Street in Pasadena across from the Kaiser Permanente medical offices, a policeman in a car suddenly pulled up alongside the curb and said he wanted to talk to me because I fitted perfectly the description of a man who had just committed a bank robbery. I politely told him he had the wrong man and I hadn't committed any bank robbery, and that I didn't know anything about it whatsoever.

The policeman then proceeded to ask me a number of questions regarding my name, residence, age, etc. I answered all of these questions politely and truthfully. He then began to repeat the questions over and over again. I answered them over and over again. He asked for my identification and I showed it to him. He asked how long I'd lived in the area, and where I was from originally. I told him. He asked what I did for a living and I told him.

Suddenly a second police car pulled alongside and I was soon surrounded by at least three or four policemen. On at least three or more separate occasions I was asked where I lived, and I told them I didn't have the exact street address but since it was only a block or two away I would show them where it was. They showed no interest what-soever in this reasonable suggestion. The policeman who had just arrived in the second car began to repeat the same questions that the policeman in the first car had asked. I told him I'd already answered those questions. I was asked for my driver's license and I told them I didn't drive.

The policemen became extremely hostile and threat-ening in their manner. They began to say among them-selves, "He's probably wanted out of state." - "You think we should arrest him?" - "Yeah, I think so, let's take him down to headquarters," etc.

Serious...

At one point early in the questioning by the first officer before the second car had arrived I was told, "This is seri-ous." This simple statement spilled the beans on the entire police operation and clearly revealed it to be the filthy stinking set up it was. If the officer really believed I had just robbed a bank, the officer would know that I damn well knew it was "serious" and he wouldn't make such a stupid statement.

Arrested...

As I stated earlier, the officers began to repeat the same questions over and over again, interspersing comments among themselves that they'd have to take me to the station. I said, "I don't know anything about this bank robbery and I've already answered your questions and I don't have to give you any further answers to the same questions." I said, "I have the right to remain silent after giving you basic information about myself." The officer, said, "Well, you're thinking of New York state. The laws are different out here."

The questions and threats to arrest me continued. I said, "I'm not answering any more questions. If you want to arrest me, arrest me - that's it." The one officer from the second car who was obviously the leader of the pack said, "Arrest him!"

Brutally Handcuffed...

I was immediately handcuffed in a brutal fashion, the police pushing my hands way, way up behind my back and causing me considerable discomfort and pain. Later I saw that the metal had torn into the flesh of both my wrists.

I was put into a police car but was unable to move in far enough for them to close the door because there is some kind of a hump in the middle of the back seat. After several attempts to shut the door by brutally pushing my right leg with his right leg, the officer finally succeeded in closing the door by pushing my leg in with the door itself. Later I saw that my right knee had turned black and blue.

False Arrest…

At one point as they were leading me into the car after they had arrested me, I saw the officer that had first approached me continue the bank robbery charade. He showed the leader of the pack officer what appeared to be a photocopy of an artist's rendition of the supposed bank robbery suspect. I also saw the picture. With the exception of the fact that we both wore beards, the picture did not look in the least bit like me. The man in the picture wore glasses, his face was completely different from mine, the hair on his head was different, etc., etc.

It was absolutely impossible to mistake me for him. And if after honestly (which was definitely not the case here) mistaking me for the man in the picture, it could not possibly take more than a few seconds at most by comparing the picture with my face to realize the mistake.

But obviously the bank robbery bit was just a lying transparent pretext for approaching and arresting me. The officers never had the slightest question in their minds that I might be the so-called "bank robber." The officer who showed him the picture said, "It looks just like him, doesn't it?" The leader of the pack officer said, "Naw, that's not him."

On the way to the police station an announcement came over the police car radio on the police band. One officer said, "That's it - they just caught the bank robber!"

Insulted...

On the way to the station, I was insulted several times, called an asshole, etc. At some point (perhaps it was already at the jailhouse) the police said, if I wasn't such an asshole they wouldn't have arrested me. After we got to the police station and I got out of the car, I said, "Well, you've got the bank robber. What do you want with me now? He said, "We just want to talk to you inside." I said, "About what?" Answer - "Let's just talk inside." Inside they began repeating the same questions again. I was seated and still had my hands handcuffed behind my back. When I refused to give them any more information I was physically attacked.

Choked...

The leader of the pack officer said, "We want to find out what this is all about!" Without any provocation of any kind on my part, he grabbed my throat with one hand and started choking me by the neck, pushing me backward in the chair (throughout all this "interrogation," savagery and physical assault, I was seated and with my hands handcuffed behind my back) and putting his face close up to mine grimaced and shouted, "Talk!"

As he was choking me a woman who apparently worked there walked by. She quickly turned her head to the left to look in the room to see what the commotion was all about. When she saw that I was being choked by the neck she quickly turned her head away and continued walking down the hallway. She obviously didn't want to see something she shouldn't see and get involved on my behalf to save my life - it could cost her her job, you know. The crazed officer who was choking me realized he'd been a little careless and with his hand still on my neck choking me he told another cop to close the door. The choking episode continued for perhaps about a total of 10 or 20 seconds. When the crazed officer saw that I refused to talk or cringe and whine and beg for mercy, he released my throat and jumped back with a fearful look in his face like he'd just seen a ghost.

I said, "I don't believe this - being choked by the neck with my hands handcuffed behind my back by a policeman at the station to get me to talk. I thought this was only in the comic books!" A couple of the officers chuckled at my naiveté. The leader of the pack crazed officer snapped, "Book him!" and took off.

Assailant Description…

I think just for the record it is appropriate to physically describe the officer who choked me since I don't know his name. He's, I'd say, in his late thirties or early forties, with kind of two-toned hair that stands up kind of prickly or goes straight back. One part of the hair in front seems brown and the other blond or gray. He's thin and lanky and fairly tall. He's hyper-aggressive, like a little dog who barks and snaps a lot and bares his teeth. He is also quite vicious.

I believe this should be more than sufficient to pin down the name and identity of this officer. I described him thusly to someone who is familiar with the Pasadena police and he immediately knew who I was talking about although he didn't recall the name offhand. I'm sure I could easily recognize him if I saw him again. For example I could easily pick him out of a police lineup.

Stark Naked…

After this I was taken upstairs to the jail part of the police department. One of the officers who arrested me said to the man behind the desk, "We've got him on the identity" or "We've got him on the identity thing." When I told the man at the desk there who wanted me to answer questions that I had just been choked by the neck down-stairs, he sarcastically sniggered, "Aw, they wouldn't do that, uh, uh, they're good men. I know them, they'd never do that," and he sneered. When I refused to answer any more questions and after they had taken all my personal belongings, I was led to a cell and they forced me to strip completely naked and leave all my clothes outside the cell. When I stripped down to my jockey mesh shorts, I said, "This too?" referring to my underpants, and the jailer nodded and said, "Yes." I took my underpants off and gave it to him also.

No Phone Call...

I was refused the right to make a phone call.

After the desk officer joker locked the door of the cell he snickered, "The phone's on the wall." Of course, there was no phone there.

Horror Cell...

The cell had no sheets, no bed, no mattress, no covers - absolutely nothing except a few thin pieces of toilet paper. I was forced to lie stark naked on a painted metal bunk with little round holes in it everywhere. After a very short period of time, of course, this became unbearable and excruciatingly uncomfortable and painful. To add to my discomfort the light was turned on in the cell. I was kept locked up in that cell until some time Wednesday morning, May 27, when I was transferred to another cell that made my first cell seem like a picnic.

Isolation & Torture...

This cell was a kind of isolation cell. Way in the far corner overlooking the street, it had two windows on different walls of the room, both windows being open. The cell door was completely solid with no opening except a one-way peep hole for the jailers to look in. The room was extremely drafty and cold and dank.

Of course, my suffering in this room was completely horrendous and unbearable, being still stripped stark naked as I was. My body and flesh are still in pain and agony from this gruesome and cruel experience as I write these lines about 8 or 10 days later. I was left in there to freeze to death or die from exposure.

I shouted to numerous passersby in the street to call a certain telephone number and to tell them that I was being tortured to death in the Pasadena police station, which was absolutely the truth.

In addition to all of the pain and torment I felt from the cold, the draftiness, and lack of clothes, at about noon-time the room became extremely noisy from the street traffic. By any standards, the decibel level was such as could easily cause permanent hearing damage. Also, at intervals, trains would rumble by at extremely loud noise levels. And of course being imprisoned in the room above city traffic, the smog level was even worse than normal.

I was left for many hours on end isolated in this room without anyone coming to the door or into the room to talk to me.

I had once read a book on brainwashing and it told how in North Korea, captured American G.I.'s during the Korean war were placed in rooms and forced to sleep on freezing blocks of ice. But I simply could not believe that here in the "civilized" U.S., a somewhat modified and slower (though equally deadly) treatment was being applied by American citizens to another American citizen. And all this without a trial, without any accusations being made against me, etc. My crime was simply that I had nothing more to say to these gangster police officers of Pasadena!!! Incredible, but true.

After I had been tortured in this room for some time, some jailers came in and told me that if I'd talk to them and give them more information, they'd give me my clothes back, and that I was being punished for my "attitude." They said they couldn't take me down to the court to see the judge until the arrest form had been all filled out. They said the judge wouldn't even see me until then. I reminded them that I'd been choked by the neck and that

I had nothing more to say to them, and that I'd do my talking to the judge.

Mental Hospital...

They told me that they might have to send me to a mental institution for observation. They asked me what year it was, what month it was, etc. I easily answered these stupid questions.

I told them again and again I wanted to make a phone call. I was refused. I was told, "You're not going to make a phone call or see the judge until we get the information we want." Numerous times I was bargained with, that they'd give me my clothes back if I'd give them the information they wanted.

Starving & Freezing...

I was denied food for some 24 hours or so straight. I told them they were starving and freezing me to death. They said, "Die! We hope you do. You can die for all I care," etc.

Inside Mattress...

In order to save my life and to try to get out of the cold and draft, I crawled inside the linoleum covered plastic mattress. A jailer looked in through the peep hole and asked me what I was doing inside the mattress. I told him I was trying to get out of the cold. He said I had destroyed prison property by doing so. So I said, "What do you want me to do - quietly freeze to death to make you happy?" He said, "Yes, I hope you do freeze to death, I don't care." I was told, "That's another charge against you - destroying prison property." He told me to get out of the mattress. I said, "Give me my clothes and I will." He left.

Incidentally, I didn't destroy the mattress or any other prison property. The mattress had already been opened by somebody else before me. Much later, just before my release from that hell hole - the Pasadena jailhouse - I was transferred to another cell (for many prisoners) and saw several more of these particular mattresses they have up there. They were all in good condition and sewed up. I looked them over and estimate that it would be extremely difficult - virtually impossible - to open them up without a knife or sharp cutting object of some kind. I suppose they are made that way deliberately. And, of course, I had no knife or any other object of any kind in my isolation cell.

The charge that I destroyed the mattress is totally laughable because the mattress was my only chance to even partially try to get out of the cold, dankness and draftiness. It would have made absolutely no sense whatever for me to destroy it.

However, I would add that in order to save my life from the freezing cold I would have been fully justified in destroying one or even a thousand of those mattresses, or even destroying the entirety of the prison. If one is allowed to kill in self defense, how much more should he be allowed to destroy a cheap prison mattress to save his life. Although I reiterate I did not destroy said mattress or anything else in the jailhouse.

On numerous occasions I was threatened with being sent to a mental hospital for observation. I was told if I didn't stop screaming they were going to come into the cell and stuff a towel or rag in my mouth to shut me up. I told the jailer if he did I would smash his blankety-blank head off. I also added that I hadn't eaten all day.

T.V. Dinner...

The next thing I knew I was brought my first food for over 24 hours, which shows you never know what to expect next in a madhouse. It consisted of two T.V. dinners and a little bit of a soft drink. I ate one T.V. dinner and decided to save the other one for later since the "room service" was so irregular. A while later, however, I was transferred back to the cell they'd put me in originally when I first came to the jailhouse. I asked the jailer to let me take the other T.V. dinner with me but he refused permission.

No Water...

The cell they returned me to now had no running water. They claimed they just couldn't understand it; "the water and plumbing had worked just fine in there before," - chuckle, chuckle. After I was returned to this cell for what seemed like a very long time - some ten hours or so or perhaps more - I became very, very thirsty, having had only a small amount of water to drink since my arrival. (Of course, how could I know they would later deny me even this basic necessity?)

Sick Cop...

I told them I was hungry and especially thirsty, and that there was no running water in my cell. Just to make doubly sure I didn't get any water to drink, the toilet was full of urine. They either laughed, made snide remarks, ignored me, or told me I was being "punished" for my attitude. Finally, after countless repeated requests for water, a big, tall blond or red-headed cop came over to my cell window and smiled in and said, "Here, I've got some water for you." Something about his "friendly" laughing attitude made me suspicious, and I said, "Open the door and bring it in - I can't take it through the steel mesh opening. It's too small, how can I get it?"

He answered, "You ever hear of a straw? Come here, I'll give it to you through a straw." I half suspected something was up and as I got up out of the bunk I found I was right - he threw the water all over my back and on the metal bunk and on the small pieces of toilet paper I had placed on the metal bunk to make it ever so slightly softer. The big cop walked away laughing hysterically. He was saying to his jailer officer buddies, "Did you see that? Ha, ha, ha!" I said, "You're really sick, only a sick person would do that." He said, "I know it, ha, ha, ha, that's why they hired me, ha, ha, ha, ha!" This is typical of the kind of sicko's and whacko's who run the Pasadena jailhouse and work for the Pasadena police force.

Police Indecency...

I should also add that in the jailhouse there are lady jailers and female prisoners. The female jailers were constantly walking past my cell and could see right into it and see me stark naked. The same for women prisoners. I remember at least one colored young lady prisoner being led past my cell. Where is the decorum and decency in all this? Also, I was twice forced to walk stark naked down the hallway of the jailhouse when I was transferred to different cells, in plain view of all.

Threats...

Later I was threatened again with being sent to a mental hospital for 30 days observation, then I'd be sent back here, and he said something about Norwalk, or Norfolk. Numerous times I told them I thought I had the constitutional right under the fifth amendment to remain silent. They replied, "No, not until you give us the information we want." I said, "You mean you're just going to keep me here forever, incommunicado until I talk?" "That's right," was the answer. "Here, or we'll send you to a mental hospital. You're obviously a very sick person."

Finally some time on Thursday morning, May 28th, I received my breakfast, which consisted of a few tablespoons of milk, a small carton of sugar coated cornflakes, and a canned peach slice. This was the first liquid I had had in a very long time.

Same Questions & Answers...

A man who said he was the chief jailer there, an older white-haired cop, told me that the reason my clothes were taken away from me was that I might use them to commit suicide since I was obviously crazy. I said, "Well, have somebody watch me then." Answer - silence. Then he promised to send me to the judge that morning if I'd answer just five questions. I asked him to tell me the five questions (it turned out to be six) in advance and I'd consider it.

The six questions were:

#1. Your name

#2. Your place of birth

#3. Your date of birth

#4. Your address

#5. Your height

#6. Your weight

I answered the questions and some time later was given my clothes back. I got dressed and was transferred to a big cell with several other prisoners.

Police Crimes...

The police now for the first time answered my questions about what the charges were. They told me the charges against me were interfering with the duties of an officer. (I joked to some of the other prisoners that I was being charged with "interfering with the crimes of an officer.")

I was also told that I had a second charge against me now I was brought into the jail, i.e., destruction of prison property, namely a prison mattress. The old white-haired chief told me the mattress cost $80.00 new. "You're going to be charged with destruction of prison property for getting in that mattress." They also told me that bail was set at $ 500.00 on each count, for a grand total of $ 1,000.00 (one thousand dollars) cash.

I told the head jailer that now I wanted to see the judge as he'd promised. He broke his word and said that there'd now developed some problem and that I wouldn't be able to see the judge today, that I'd have to wait until tomorrow for that.

Phone Call...

I was allowed to make phone calls from the public pay phone in this new cell. I called someone and told them the situation, that I'd been arrested, choked by the neck, and held in the Pasadena jailhouse incommunicado and stark naked for the past 48 hours or so, etc. The person was shocked but relieved to hear from me since naturally the person had been very worried about my disappearance.

Fingerprints...

After the person came down to the jailhouse and put up the bail money, I was taken to a special room for a mug shot and to be fingerprinted. I asked the head jailer what if I refused to be fingerprinted, what would he do? He said they'd break every bone in my hands if they had to to get those fingerprints.

Signed Unread...

After the mug shot and the fingerprinting, thumb printing, hand printing, palm printing, etc., I was told to sign numerous documents, perhaps as many as 10 or more. I told the chief jailer that I like to read documents before I sign them. He insisted that I just sign them.

I reiterated my previous statement and started to read them. He demanded that I sign the documents at once without giving me time to even partially glance at them. He covered the document with his hand and arm and said, "All that concerns you is this here part at the bottom of the page," indicating what looked like a kind of stamp or form letter part of certain words which I did not have time to read either.

Having had little or no sleep for over two days and suffering from exhaustion, and knowing that a document signed under physical duress has no validity in law, and being in a hurry to get out of that damn hell hole, I signed the documents without reading them. I was not allowed to read them.

For all I know I signed a confession that I killed 20 Pasadena police officers and that I destroyed all the mattresses in the entire jailhouse and then tore the jailhouse down with my bare hands.

No Written Charges...

The charges made against me until now, two weeks later, are still all verbal. I have received no written accusation of any charges against me whatsoever. All they gave was two receipts for $500.00 bail on each one. No accusations on them, and as a matter of fact no clear command to appear anywhere.

(No) Money Back...

Finally I was taken back to the desk where I had checked in at and had left my personal belongings some two days earlier. As I was putting my belongings in my pockets, I noticed that my wallet was empty of money. I remembered that when I left home that Tuesday I had nine dollars in cash and well over another dollar in change. I also distinctly remembered counting out the bills when I was checked into the jail and they took my belongings. I remembered clearly the arresting officer snickering as he counted out the bills, "Six, seven, eight, nine dollars," snicker.

So now I said to the chief jailer, "Hey, where's my money? I had ten bucks." He shouted, "No, you didn't! You had no money when you came in here! " I said, "What are you talking about? I had ten dollars." Some kind of eye communication went on between the chief jailer and the man behind the desk. The chief jailer quickly changed his attitude and asked the man behind the desk if I came in there with the money. He nodded and said, "Yes," or something, and the chief jailer quickly gave me a ten dollar bill and marked something on a piece of paper, or made as if he were marking something on a piece of paper.

Incidentally, I had given them when I checked in either a five dollar bill and four ones plus well over a dollar in change or nine ones plus well over a dollar in change

(I'm 99% sure it was the former). What happened to those bills and change is an interesting question in itself. I had previously been given three dimes by the chief jailer for my phone calls so I didn't bother arguing about the exact change that might still be due me, especially since it looked like I was actually about to get out of that hell hole.

That afternoon I was told I could go, and an electronically operated gate was opened and I took the elevator down and left the jailhouse. A while later I noticed that several pills of mine had been stolen by the police/jailers. I presume they destroyed the pills hoping to find that they were illegal. When they found nothing - well, bye-bye pills.

Sham...

Legality is a sham at the jailhouse. There are No Smoking signs everywhere, and no smoking is rigidly enforced - for the prisoners. But I noticed a light-skinned colored cop/jailer smoking whenever he pleased.

Numerous interesting and curious questions arise regarding why I was stopped by the policeman as "a bank robbery suspect." The first officer who stopped me said, "There's just been a bank robbery...," etc. Then a few minutes later in the police car on the way to the police station, an officer told me that they'd just picked up the bank robber. My question is how could the police have had a

photocopy of an artist's rendition of what the bank robbery suspect looked like in the short time that presumably
had occurred between the time of the bank robbery and
the time the first officer (photocopy of the artist's rendition
of the bank robber in hand) had approached me?

Unasked Questions...

Why wasn't I asked any questions about the bank robbery if that were the real reason I was stopped? I was never
asked where I'd been the last few minutes, never told what
bank had been robbed, how much had been taken, etc.
I was not out of breath from running, had no weapon,
only a little cash on me. They never bothered to check my
face against that of the artist's rendition of the bank robber
until after I was already arrested. To say the whole thing
stinks and is a frame up and set up is to put it mildly.

True Events...

The foregoing text was written between about June 5
and June 8, 1981, then later typed, edited, slightly revised,
corrected, etc. However, no attempt has been made to bring
it up to date or to incorporate later information or events,
etc. It is a brief outline, a hastily written sketch, of the
horrendous and incredible but absolutely true events that
occurred to me in my life between about 2:00 p.m. Tuesday,
May 26, 1981, and about 1:30 p.m. Thursday, May 28,

1981. I do not pretend that this is literature. However, it is absolutely accurate in all the main points, at least a thousand times more accurate and truthful than anything you will hear from the other side - i.e., the policemen and the jailers and all the rest of the law enforcement authorities. Perhaps in the future when I have more time to devote to it I will write a revised and expanded and even more accurate and painstakingly written account of these events.

Sincerely,

Robert D. James

Robert D. James (professionally known
as Robert J. Fischer or Bobby Fischer,
The World Chess Champion)

THE MORALS OF CHESS
BY BENJAMIN FRANKLIN

Sir,

Playing at Chess, is the most ancient and the most universal game known among men; for its original is beyond the memory of history, and it has, for numberless ages, been the amusement of all the civilized nations of Asia, the Persians, the Indians, and the Chinese. Europe has had it above 1000 years; the Spaniards have spread it over their part of America, and it begins lately to make its appearance in these northern states. It is so interesting in itself, as not to need the view of gain to induce engaging in it; and thence it is never played for money. Those, therefore, who have leisure for such diversions, cannot find one that is more *innocent*; and the following piece, written with a view to correct (among a few young friends) some little improprieties in the practice of it, shows at the same time, that it may, in its effects on the mind, be not merely *innocent,* but *advantageous,* to the vanquished as well as to the victor.

The MORALS of CHESS.

The game of Chess is not merely an idle amusement. Several very valuable qualities of the mind, useful in the course of human life, are to be acquired or strengthened by it, so as to become habits, ready on all occasions. For life is a kind of chess, in which we have often points to gain, and competitors or adversaries to contend with, and in which there is a vast variety of good and ill events, that are, in some degree, the effects of prudence or the want of it. By playing at chess, then, we may learn:

1. *Foresight,* which looks a little into futurity, and considers the consequences that may attend an action: for it is continually occurring to the player, "If I move this piece, what will be the advantages of my new situation? What use can my adversary make of it to annoy me? What other moves can I make to support it, and to defend myself from his attacks?

2. *Circumspection,* which surveys the whole chess-board, or scene of action, the relations of the several pieces and situations, the dangers they are respectively exposed to, the several possibilities of their aiding each other; the probabilities that the adversary may make this or that move, and attack this or the other piece; and what different means can be used to avoid his stroke, or turn its consequences against him.

3. *Caution,* not to make our moves too hastily. This habit is best acquired by observing strictly the laws of the game, such as, *if you touch a piece, you must move it somewhere; if you set it down, you must let it stand.* And it is therefore best that these rules should be observed, as the game thereby becomes more the image of human life, and particularly of war; in which, if you have incautiously put yourself into a bad and dangerous position, you cannot obtain your enemy's leave to withdraw your troops, and place them more securely; but you must abide all the consequences of your rashness.

And, *lastly,* we learn by chess the habit of *not being discouraged* by *present* bad appearences in the state of our affairs, the habit of *hoping for a favourable change,* and that of *persevering in the search of resources.* The game is so full of events, there is such a variety of turns in it, the fortune of it is so subject to sudden vicissitudes, and one so frequently, after long contemplation, discovers the means of extricating one's self from a supposed insurmountable difficulty, that one is encouraged to continue the contest to the last, in hopes of victory by our own skill, or, at least, of giving a *stale mate,* by the negligence of our adversary. And whoever considers, what in chess he often sees instances of, that particular pieces of success are apt to produce *presumption,* and its consequent, inattention, by which more is afterwards lost than was gained by the preceding advantage;

while misfortunes produce more care and attention, by which the loss may be recovered, will learn not to be too much discouraged by the present success of his adversary, nor to despair of final good fortune, upon every little check he receives in the pursuit of it.

That we may, therefore, be induced more frequently to chuse this beneficial amusement, in preference to others which are not attended with the same advantages, every circumstance, that may increase the pleasure of it, should be regarded; and every action or word that is unfair, disrespectful, or that in any way may give uneasiness, should be avoided, as contrary to the immediate intention of both the players, which is to pass the time agreeably.

Therefore, 1st. If it is agreed to play according to the strict rules, then those rules are to be exactly observed by both parties; and should not be insisted on for one side, while deviated from by the other: for this is not equitable.

2. If it is agreed not to observe the rules exactly, but one party demands indulgencies, he should then be as willing to allow them to the other.

3. No false move should ever be made to extricate yourself out of a difficulty, or to gain an advantage. There can be no pleasure in playing with a person once detected in such unfair practice.

4. If your adversary is long in playing, you ought not to hurry him, or express any uneasiness at his delay. You should not sing, nor whistle, nor look at your watch, nor take up a book to read, nor make a tapping with your feet on the floor, or with your fingers on the table, nor do anything that may disturb his attention. For all these things displease. And they do not show your skill in playing, but your craftiness or your rudeness.

5. You ought not to endeavour to amuse and deceive your adversary, by pretending to have made bad moves, and saying you have now lost the game, in order to make him secure and careless, and inattentive to your schemes; for this is fraud, and deceit, not skill in the game.

6. You must not, when you have gained a victory, use any triumphing or insulting expression, nor show too much pleasure; but endeavour to console your adversary, and make him less dissatisfied with himself by every kind and civil expression, that may be used with truth, such as, You understand the game better than I, but you are a little inattentive; or, You play too fast; or, You had the best of the game but something happened to divert your thoughts, and that turned it in my favour.

7. If you are a spectator, while others play, observe the most perfect silence. For if you give advice, you offend both parties; him, against whom you give it,

because it may cause the loss of his game; him, in whose favour you give it, because, though it be good, and he follows it, he loses the pleasure he might have had, if you had permitted him to think till it occurred to himself. Even after a move or moves, you must not, by replacing the pieces, shew how it might have been played better: for that displeases, and may occasion disputes or doubts about their true situation. All talking to the players, lessens or diverts their attention, and is therefore unpleasing; nor should you give the least hint to either party, by any kind of noise or motion.— If you do, you are unworthy to be a spectator.— If you have a mind to exercise or show your judgments, do it in playing your own game when you have an opportunity, not in criticising or meddling with, or counselling, the play of others.

Lastly. If the game is not to be played rigorously, according to the rules above mentioned, then moderate your desire of victory over your adversary, and be pleased with one over yourself. Snatch not eagerly at every advantage offered by his unskilfulness or inattention; but point out to him kindly that by such a move he places or leaves a piece in danger and unsupported; that by another he will put his king in a dangerous situation, etc. By this generous civility (so opposite to the unfairness above forbidden) you may indeed happen to lose the game to your opponent, but you will win what is better, his esteem, his respect, and his affection; together with the silent approbation and good will of impartial spectators.

Robert D. James

B. Franklin

Jon Rock

ALSO BY J. M. ROCK:
DEATH BY SOCIALISM

ISBN Paperback:
979-8-218-37228-6
ISBN Hardcover:
979-8-9901552-0-6

Introduction:

Every year, there is a list of the world's top causes of death.

The list ordinarily includes heart disease, stroke, pulmonary disease, lung cancer, tuberculosis, and malaria, among others.

However, there is one cause of death that is conspicuously absent from this list; one that has claimed more than one hundred million lives over the past century alone, and one that has left countless millions of lives and families in shambles.

You will not find this cause of death listed on any coroner's reports. You will not find any laboratories researching a cure. There are no fundraisers or public awareness campaigns around it. You will not even find a passing mention of it in any of the newspapers. It is the most ruthless of serial killers, and yet it never has its day in court. More than people, this cause of death has claimed entire civilizations.

It is the most silent of killers: it is *Death by Socialism*.